W0232670

CENTRAL TIME

CENTRAL TIME

POEMS 2006–2014

RANJIT HOSKOTE

PENGUIN
VIKING
An imprint of Penguin Random House

VIKING

USA | Canada | UK | Ireland | Australia
New Zealand | India | South Africa | China | Singapore

Viking is part of the Penguin Random House group of companies
whose addresses can be found at global.penguinrandomhouse.com

Published by Penguin Random House India Pvt. Ltd
4th Floor, Capital Tower 1, MG Road,
Gurugram 122 002, Haryana, India

Penguin
Random House
India

First published in Viking by Penguin Books India 2014

10 9 8 7 6 5 4 3 2

ISBN 9780670086818

Typeset in Garamond Regular by SÜRYA, New Delhi
Printed at Replika Press Pvt. Ltd, India

www.penguin.co.in

MIX
Paper from
responsible sources
FSC® C016779

This is a legitimate digitally printed version of the book and therefore might not
have certain extra finishing on the cover.

For Nancy

The skilled restorer of porcelain will collect not only the visible chips of a broken pot but also the dust on the table where it rested

Richard Sennett

Contents

I Zoetrope

II The Pilot's Almanac

III   Gravity Leaps to the Eye

IV   The Existence Certificate

V   The Institute of Silence

I

Zoetrope

Platform Directions

Hamburger Bahnhof, Berlin

Here's how you solve the riddles this train station poses
when you come in from the sun, wristwatch stopped,
looking for shade under cool timetables.

Start by walking around. Stare at a pyramid
you cannot enter. Look through an igloo
made of glass and numbers.

Or test the runway laid out for a plane
that could never take off.
It taxies around a circle of broken stones.

Now try the ramp that leads to a library
of lead books, their pages stapled down
and a strong lens provided

to blur the missing author's words.
Someone's marked their favourite passages
with dried poppy seeds.

You're pulling on your coat, hefting your rucksack.
But where's the rush, my friend?
Have a cappuccino while you wait.

You can take your time at this station.
No train stops here, no train ever leaves.

To the Sanskrit Poets

Leave something behind: a trace of cloud
on a plate, a pair of white birds

shot by a hunter, an emerald brooch
that a shrub snatched from a princess in flight

or the archer's last prayer, spoken minutes before
his brother's arrow found his throat.

Leave us these threads to unravel, embroider:
secret messages inked in white

on white beneath the unsettled weeks
of postcards and air letters

that jam the mailbox while we're away.
Leave us the jigsaw of previous lives.

Giant Malabar Squirrel

Anuradhapura

Large and motionless as a jackfruit about to fall,
he hung off the banyan for minutes,
head pointing earthward,
unmindful of gravity
and the body's natural justice.
Brush-tailed ambassador of the higher branches:
his back unblessed by the triple stripe
of Rama's grateful fingers, his stare
a declaration of war.

He ignored the shelled nuts and coconut flesh
that we held out, waited for us to back off,
climb back on the bus that had brought us there.
Through our tinted windows
we saw him blur down the bark and spring,
forepaws gripping the earth,
nostrils dilated for hostile smells.

Behind his bristling tail the stupa rose
chalk-white, ripe in the centre of our eyes,
blinding at noon.

Occupying a Cold Country

No locks on the doors
and the natives will have to be invented.
We draw back the bolts of our frosted breath:
settlers, arriving through the water
of dissolving windowpanes,
rushes beating against our faces.

Numbers

A day pruned of its branches, scorched by the nomad's fire, the sun a howl in the sky's throat. The graves are numbered, without verses or seasons to ground them. The caretaker has left a list behind. Before the war, this used to be

an aerodrome, says the engineer, kneeling. Sand peppers his sleeves as he matches numbers to names. Faces form at his fingertips. The list grows in the heat, the hills circle his head. He looks up, eyes creased against the sun. It begins to drizzle.

Gargoyle, Notre Dame

for Guy and Florence

Staggering up the steep, tight-wound steps,
you swallow the sky in a wide breath,
panting, tongue out like a dog's.
Chin in palm, you hunch over the parapet,
look down, and find him at your elbow,
panting, chin in palm, tongue out like a dog's,
hunched over the parapet, looking down
at the spiralling distance you have come.

Your mimic, twin in labour. Except he's as old
as the cathedral, and hewn in stone.
The masons must have enjoyed crafting
his pointed ears and umbrella wings.
He looks, and you look with him, at the square
where children are playing hopscotch
around the bronze star set in the paving:
the zero point where all roads start,
all journeys end.

You salute, he holds his peace.
You shoulder your rucksack and climb on
to the belfry, hoping to catch
the grace of a carillon this afternoon.
He stays, his eyes fixed on the star and the streets
that branch out from the island's heart.
He will cross the bridge of the seasons alone,
laughing, sobbing, constant at his post,
too strong for the pilgrim chain-gangs
that strain and push to get past him:

stone wings folded, last angel, he's stapled to the view.

Painter Talking to Flowers

in memoriam: Bhupen Khakhar (1934–2003)

Two feet from where our jeep drew mud
from the monsoon-rutted road, he stood
talking to the yellow flowers pricked out
against the marching khaki wall of shrubs
behind which the airstrip crouched,
its low growl muffled beneath the hood
of an eat-shoot-and-sleep routine.

Only this man praying at the highway's edge
could hear the planes take off and land.
To the flowers, his love was clear as day:
he floated above the iron-bound hedge,
dodged watchtowers, gagged on the spiky taste
of a metal creeper growing wild. It overran
the city's roofs. We drove on, he framed his scene.

The golden rain of the end had begun to fall
when the city locked him in a frieze
of dead lamps, blind walls, gates with sprung claws.
By fading light, he looked hard at the old maw
and while his breath emptied to a final pause,
he grinned and painted the parachute trees
in the mildewed sepias of autumn.

Border Post

Where someone's gouged a brick from the wall,
a bicycle leans and listens to the light.

One hand claps at air until another hand answers:
a column of breath roots itself in the hushed soil.

The Grammarian's Farewell to Language

Recalled in guilt's tenor, that night returns.
Your ear, though numbed by rush-hour traffic,
cannot muffle its sound, which is the sound
of a sea growling deep within a shell.
It carries the freight
of a forgiveness you cannot ask.
Logic does not help you
nor the proper phrase.
Whatever the word does,
it gets there late.

Electronic Nocturne

The TV goes dead, killing all the newscasters.
Go, loud satraps of the night,
leave us alone with darkness and ourselves.

Length in Running Feet

for Rahul Mehrotra

In Corjuem, where the river has changed sides
after every battle, and every stone bears two signatures,
you balance your thoughts on a forked stick.

Space turns slowly into place
as you patch the hills
with maps and elevations:
the pavilion is a flap of sky, the wall
travels across the hills to meet the sun,
the screen is a veil of light
between the forest's darkness and the house.

The wall strides on through the shrubbery,
cutting through the forest; and whoever looks
through the windows sees windows
reflecting his face in a hundred skies.
Gruff basalt and tight-lipped laterite
turn voluble as you free-hand a curve
across the horizon, capture us in anecdotes.

Stretching a roof across the cliff,
you've unlatched windows in an air that's crusting
into eaves, corners, niches;
unbolted doors so they can frame
the cooling sun at nightfall.
What you create is not place
but the legend of place.

The Invention of the Senses

for Masaki Fujihata

Touch crosses the small distances of this room,
caressing a pebble, smoothing a ruffled curtain.
When you rest your hand on this ebony table,
a book floats to the surface, opens to page one.
Run your fingers along the paper, the edge, the spine,
and a lamp begins to glow faintly in a corner.

Touch unlocks the closed and private cells:
unlike the voice, its ends are not gregarious.
Searching alone, it brings home what you've lost:
open your hands in a shallow fan
of ten fingers, and a door clicks open,
a child looks through.

Explorer

Boots burst, sleds gone astray, samoyeds baying,
he's locked in ice.

More than anyone else in the world this afternoon,
he needs the consolation of arrival:
dry earth, a house in a laburnum grove,
soft sheets and a fire
to warm his hands,
a dog to nuzzle his face.
Any dream of home to ward off the floes
that drift towards him, blocking every direction
on his lost compass.

The sun has flared a deep red-orange,
the colour of a beloved word
he was trying to recall. It escapes him.
Coursing in his bloodstream, the poison of time
swims from organ to organ.
His mind, tired recruit to the staying game,
now loses the heft and smell of words.
All but white, which dances between him
and the blotted sun.

Gravity cannot hold him.
He is ready to travel.

Canticle for a Bridge

A waver in the glass.
Heliotrope petals on the river.
He touches her drawings again.

Ten years have passed
since the bridge-builder buried his bride.
His spans are silent as rock

but the waters echo
with the flapping of a thousand wings.
Speak to me, he says,

in one tongue only.

Conspiracies

in memoriam: Dom Moraes (1938–2004)

This forest is for real, as are its natives,
each one the genuine article.
The centaur who's just lost his throne.
The hunchback who has a bone to pick
with the dwarf who is
an agent provocateur.
The clown who has an axe to grind
and the cat who keeps the records
and never sleeps.

~

The centaur falls silent in the noose,
his voice clotted around its last command.
The dwarf raises his cudgel in triumph.

At a nod from the hunchback, the clown
hacks off the dwarf's head.
The soundtrack goes silent: no shriek rings out
among the trees, or the remaindered lots of buildings
beyond. The mouth that spelled riot and uprising
is a clipped line of blood.

The clown mops his brow, pushes back
his dishevelled red hair.
He flips the sun that the hunchback hands him,
shoves it deep into his greasy pocket.

The cat, prowling through the forest,
hears a cannonade go off
in the centaur's head
as he swings.

To conspire is to breathe together,
whispers the hunchback, a literary sort.
The delirium fades, the toys fall back
in their tin box. A boy comes in

to pick up the pieces.

Travelling Light

for Baiju Parthan

Eat slowly. Read what you can by available light.
Take nothing with you
except the sky stencilled in the window

to picture the next stage in this journey
that will carry you past the poplars of home,
past scrub and palms to the unyielding sea.

And when the train stops at the last beach,
forget the harmony of the spheres
that you thought to find in hard things and fluent.

Put your bag down and look
at the reef that gashes
through the ocean

and the meteors that light up
the moon's silences.

Nazm

for Nancy

Our lives are voices in two heads.
The rest is background music.

~

In this city of high walls, the scores of abandoned music
flutter in the streets and my torn-out Aztec heart
comes to rest, a blind girl's paperweight.

~

Blindfold palmist, you've stitched our hands together,
completing accounts that the waking mind abandoned
to the faultless needlework of dream.

~

We lie embroidered on the mimosa.
I need no gauge of motives to tell me
why it has rained.

~

Clouds darken the windows, the lamps are lit.
You carry the incense from room to room.
I flare briefly, then go out,
a lamp you lit and forgot to trim.

~

Raw colours grate against the mind's palette.
The mirror promises only the dark.
The eyes that have glowed would rest on the mirror,
smoky lamps afloat on a clouded stream.

~

Forget the star maps of the Old Kingdom.
Dress yourself in night.
Trust me:
our hands can see in the dark.

Still Life

The sliced apple
has elephants' eyes for pips:

they stare up at the knife
that has brought them to life.

Coda

The door's frozen
like a stag in the glare of a headlight.

You won't find me here again:
the phone will ring in an empty room.
The pigeons will build their nests in a roof
that needs mending, its tiles cracked,
its dormers jammed in their frames.

Sometimes, I mourn
for the child I used to be.

Shaman

I am outside the mystery, the boy thinks,
his eyes frozen on the lilac cloud

that hovers above him, the backcloth apricot sky
soundless. The cloud's wings beat low,

tousling his hair, wetting his eyes,
opening his mouth. After it has melted

in rain, in thunder, this cloud, the boy
will find it again, veined and marbled on his tongue.

II

The Pilot's Almanac

Rain

We are nothing but water, you said,
turning back from where the sun set sail
this evening. The wind rushed through us,
reporting to night's bivouac.

It's raining daggers. I'll wake up drenched,
skin bruised, eyes stung by the flute
that keeps the oblong hours of sleep.
Come back, trace me to my deep

hiding place behind ragged nerve
and stupored vein. There's no refrain
but this to this song of first lines,
the one line running over:

my love, my love is as real
as tonight's rain.

Cutting Device

Richard Serra

You've landed in fog on a clear day.

The field widens when you test it with your feet. Look out for the edge, the instructor said, it's hidden in the turf.

Walk around, feet sinking in with every step. Crouch. Wait for your hands to wake up. Find balance.

You fumble in your coat pocket for a dog-eared sketchbook: to touch, to raise, to drop, to mould, to find.

You see the edge only after you've burned it with your arctic fingers.

Your eyes hack it out of the turf. Watch the running curve they make, jaguar slope against the dream-slowed earth.

You cannot remove yourself from this landscape. You cannot look back.

Where would you go, migrant heart, if they sent you?

The Collector of Meteor Dust

'Moon Winding Works': shop sign, Tardeo, Central Bombay, c. 1989

I make the moon happen. It blows up, fades,
bites roundels from heaven's blackout at my command.
I trick the planets into shape. Without me, you'd have
chunks of ice phantasming through space
on slipstreams, drifting out of range
across an ocean numb to the naked eye's sounding,
depth painted on velvet depth, such distances: distances
across which I stretch a net of chain-linked stars
to harbour fugitive ships, berserk and unwelcome
at the earth's tidy waterfronts.

The sky in my head is bruised by criss-cross tracers.
Fall to your knees, mariners, kneel, mourn and honour
the planets that escaped while my cunning slept.
Tomorrow's another night: I'll collect my toll
of meteor dust, make the moon happen, blow up, fade.
I wind all things up, give them names
and beginnings that haunt them to the end.

The Postman's Last Song for the Moon

for Jeet Thayil

You glide in plain view, gravity's nearest slave,
floating outside our windows, just out of reach,
an ice fruit we'd love to pluck
from the sky's jet branches.
What stops us is we know
the tides would roar and lunge, break their contract if we did:
wall-high waves rushing houses and stores, vaulting over gates,
an army of madmen dancing on drowned asphalt.

Rain-wrapped, fog-tangled, how easily we forget
oceans that have dried and shrunk
to ravines where the eye never settles,
the heart now never goes. Like the Sea of Tranquillity:
so wildly utopian we gave it to you,
tattooed it on your skin's acceptance.
Safe behind glass and our chartreuse curtains,
we watch it float by on full-moon nights and smile.

The mortgage of our nights and days is so quickly claimed.
You measure breath in the centuries it takes
to carve a pensive ellipse through space.
Messages conveyed, you dip below mouldy clouds
or submit with reluctance to an eclipse,
never more than half deciphered.
You keep your dark side hidden as you shine,
a riddle orbiting in the wide-open eye.

Sickle of the harvest, lantern of our last rooms!
Green moon of January nights,
you'll bark at our windows,
a dog begging for a bone
long after we've gone.
Other voices will wake up to answer:
survivors from the minefields of sleep,
they will pelt you with curses, extradite you to memory.

The Burden of History

A bird sits on a branch
of the fury tree:
a bird as big as India.

It's sleeping now.
You can see it
if you tilt your head.

It's crouched inside
the amber paperweight
on my desk:

shrunken, waiting for release.

Free Fall

Such readiness
to fall in love:
letting go, feet first
from the bomb bay,
flailing, ripping free
of cord and chute:

born-again diver
trusting to the drift of cloud,
the quirk of gale,
hoping to touch down
on stake-driven turf, tamped and burned,
its embers glowing like cats' eyes

at the heart of a forest
frosted, perfectly frozen.

The Masonry of Detail

It drives dead slow, the mind that's going nowhere.
It fixes on a ragged turquoise kite
that a boy's lost to a banyan,
a kite that clutches at life as an Andhra puppet might:
leather shaved close to translucence and shaped
into a demon who carries his world
wherever he goes, dancing foot stumped
on a palace, sun pinned to his crown and a creeper
breaking from his right shoulder.

It draws a line, the mind that's going nowhere,
to join all the blues that stream around it:
a man's shirt, caught in passing; the stripe painted
along an express train; a sari border
ripping under the toes of a woman
stumbling at the foot of the stairs;
and a duffel bag left on the platform,
cradling a bomb.

Passport

Rivers abrupt as whiplashes, mountains adamant as fathers. He had run away from home at fourteen. Now, caught up in a holding action against an autumn of muffled cannonades, Commander M. wanted to fall back. Back, as far north as his lost youth.

Do you expect to recapture Kabul? He saw clouds of dust, heaps of bricks. Sometimes, the shadow of a hawk on the hills. God is great, but Kabul exists only on television screens.

One September morning, he asked Ambassador K. to fly with him to a rearward base. *Take your passport.* K. had left it on a side table. He put down a teacup patterned with willows, rimmed in dull gold.

The door opened and two foreign journalists entered the room. One of them pointed his zoom at M. and pressed the shutter. The explosion hurled K. against a wall. Seven pieces of shrapnel lodged in the leather-bound document he had just put in his left breast pocket.

Commander M. never went home to the valley of his birth. A month later, recovering in hospital, Ambassador K. told reporters: *The Commander saved my life with a passport.* A passport for a fictional country, which covered his heart.

The Landscapist's Advice to His Apprentice

J.M.W. Turner (1775–1851)

Size up the sky. Will the wind be snapping
at your heels today? Can the stone arches hold up
under the storm's bruising?
Should the pines bend or crack in a gale?
Pull a rug over your knees, keep your eyes open.
The oaks may slip when the freshet strikes the bank.
Closer to heaven, the snow can take care of itself
but you can give the lower slopes a nudge
with a touch of cinnabar and a smudge of honey.

And don't forget to line the valleys
with an edge of verdigris, recharging your brush
as country passes into town and town
gallops towards a view of glassy lakes.
By noon, part the curtains of rain and allow
the sun's clear note to ring through your frame.
And the gypsies, peasants, slaves: don't keep them out
of your picturesque ruins. You'll find it improves
with a pungent shadow or greasy thumbprint,
your outdoor museum of fluted columns and broken friezes.

Monsoon Evening, Horniman Circle

Sitting on a park bench beneath magnolias
crowned with vespertine crows,
I hear a pen scratching away at paper
on a desk buried deep
in my neighbour's mind.

What looks like a drizzle hides a universe of lightning

that's large enough to contain
both the tomcat who's lost his regal poise
and scurries for cover,
and the girl in a maroon sweater
who dips under an awning, unsurprised.

Large enough to contain, and to kill with too much giving.

The doors and windows of my shaky house,
says Ghalib, have broken into green tendrils.
Why should I complain,
he draws his shawl closer in the rain,
when spring has visited my house?

Couple

Sharers of skin,
dreamers of one another's landscapes.

Thieves of one another's thoughts,
rivals for destiny's attention.

Convicts serving time
in the prison of one another's arms.

Savage antagonists marooned
on a planet no wider than a bed.

To Name a Sea

Honour the translator,
survivor of cadence:

struck by lightning,
he lives to tell the tale.

Rudderless, no mast:
he steers the boat of tomorrow

across a sea that has no walls.
Dip a seine in its water, you cannot hold

the water. By what name
shall we call its cresting blues?

By what name
shall we haul it in?

Strophe upon strophe
they strike us, the waves.

Mirror

Lightning hits the mirror and the people it holds.
Their silhouettes fall to the floor,
wisps of silver foil.

Alone on the wet marble,
you tap the empty glass and listen
for an echo.

Journal

for Richard Lannoy

Guessing your way by barbed light,
you come to a peak where a prophet scarred
two tablets with lightning.

Unwrap your prism and hone the sun.
Begin a more modest entry
on the matte scroll of grass.

Your journal opens in the rock-run silence
above the cliffs, its first glyphs
scored in limestone:

doors through which the early martyrs walked
down to the village, the stake, the rain of stones.

~

Stirring an ash circle with a forked rod,
you listen in the drought of sound
for the voices that drove raw-boned hands

to gouge the limestone, plough the stream.
You cannot read the world they pictured into words
or call up the gods their pictures spelled.

Shout your name. It bells out, returns.
Claim these cliffs. Your voice boomerangs.
Whatever you call it is only for now.

This bruised earth has crushed more names
than you could count.

~

The *wadi* lets you trespass.
You are lulled by noontime music.
Its false horizons take you prisoner.

Stumbling through its dry gullies,
you hear stonecutters
carving fruit for the ear:

grooved vowels, flared plosives
chiselled by wet hands. You stop, accept
these phrases of gratitude, chants of love.

Song is the only present.
Your time starts now.

Knowing Your Way Around

The palace of illusions shows no mercy
to those who ignore the sign at the gate.
Whoever slips on the plate-glass floor
sinks to the bottom of a lake.
Whoever lunges for the silk bell-rope
is bitten by a sleepless rattlesnake.
Whoever caresses the spiked shadows
that the palm fronds cast is stung.
And we few arrogant initiates,
who sip the juice of the nectarine,
stagger from the feast, poisoned.

Behind the Scenes

for Shanta Gokhale

The house lights go down and silence hangs
between death and voices.
The eye soaks up the dark and grasps
at russet hills preserved in glass,
at screens that crumple tawny memories
of desert in their accordion clasp.

The night is a soprano lifting her voice
among strangers. And the actors she knows?
They will not come tonight,
they have cast their masks aside,
they will not colour this act again
with their stilted moves and rounded speech.

Rain-rivered spaces crouch outside
the foyer. They sniff at boarded windows
and nudge at a back door left ajar.
When they rise from their haunches
to burst through the clapboard
and the moon-striped walls give way,

we shall not resist
the scorching transit of their breath.

Freehold

for Mehlli Gobhai

A gash of sunlight on a lemon door.
A cat hacked by the slatted shadow
of a screen, flicking its tail
to show it's alive
to the dripping of unseen faucets.
What can hold them together,
these partitioned moments,
straggling hours and makeshift days?
As you watch, the house falls

into place: walls standing up,
windows forming in pools,
fanlights capping tonsured doors,
a roof dripping eaves on the lawn.

Your feet sink in cloud.
The powdery shadow of a key
blesses your doorstep.

The house finds its breath again. Its past
is an abandoned line of defence.

The Book of Night

Annalist of the solar magistracy, I cannot complain.
Only under the stars' gaze can the other book be opened:

the book in which water strops its sheer knives
on grindstone summits while green lions ramp

in my pagan eye, and my tongue is healed
of the magnet word

by the copper taste of the breaking sea,
the unsealed beak of the soaring kite.

Evening Landscape

Heart, last philosopher to fall
prey to the biting intolerance of gravel:
a broken road, a dry river, a stone,
the roots and rhymes that last things are made of.
Will the historians decorate you
for all the wars you fought?
Go, heart, find sleep. There is no cure
for your wounds, no poison
to stop up your song.

The Reading

for Charles Simic

I should have burnt my shadow on a wall
to remind them I'd been there
and a tracery of leaves for luck
or good measure

and walked out on them, on that dramatic note,
into a morning of rain and green distances
best left unmapped. Or reckoned by roofs
you could pick off with a pointed stick.

But all I did was read to them from a book
nailed to a table blackened by centuries of elbows,
smiling around at my circle of listeners,
dropping my glasses casually on the last page.

I knotted my muffler very carefully before walking out
and left an apple on the table at the end.

III

Gravity Leaps to the Eye

The Archaeologist at Noon

Despite the perfection of the reflected sun
which burns the water that holds it

Despite the perfection of the bullet-holed clock
that spoke its last twelve and turned to stone

Despite the perfection of the pause between a cabbage
and the shadow it casts on the grey-tiled floor

Despite the perfection with which the creeper's roots
dig below the rock on which the house stands

You search for your true name, scrabbling in grass
that's drying to nothing in the perfection of the sun's gaze

Martyr

He sat on his haunches
in the dry fountain

skin bare, so bare
it shone like gold:

garish austerities
of the bereft.

Above him, a rain of pamphlets
from the gallows tree.

Nocturne with Lost Candle

Moss creeps up on topaz.
A wall gathers itself
from shadows.

He's a flame wavering in a curdled prism,
a moon flying in shards from an axe-blow,
an eye bursting with all it wants to see.

Not yet himself, he jumps from evening's window:
air-slapped, odour-blind, open to an atlas beyond his sparseness,
just a shudder of what he might be.

The tenancy of earth and air will print its costs
on his spine. He cannot remain dry as a fish in the mill-race
or hide the scars of his transit through glass.

He runs past the lurking trees,
white as a shirt fluttering under a stone,
ripped at the cuffs.

Desert

A fan of pigeons hovering
above a cyclist on a dirt track
with a rocket cone strapped to his pillion.

A caravan of domes
hangs in the scorched air, just within range,
before landing in the scrub.

Zero tiger of noon,
show yourself.
You couldn't fool the laziest detective.

The Birth of Statues

In this pigeon-strafed marketplace,
metered as a square distance that holds
a scatter of buskers, brindled strays
and yawning nomad storytellers,
I walk from stall to stall, closing the lids
of jars and eyes. The wind has carried enough:
just a whiff, not more, of crushed almonds.
Soon, the truckers will be ready to load.
The genies are curled up, their limbs made perfect
in an image of sleep.

Bearings

for Michael Krüger

I would go back in time to trawl
these lucid particulars from the tarred drift-tide:
the yellow butterfly poised like a pair
of palms in prayer;
the star climbing to sainthood
at the silver oak's zenith;
the wasp boring its sawdust martyr heart
into the painted window frame;
the full moon, delicious as a flower
pricked by the needle of lyric.

Shuttling between was and is, will I find them there,
unchanged, arranged as bearings, which first came
as chance beats in a music of surprise?
And will I get there before it's too late
to guess at whole systems of weather
that ride the oceans inside our heads
while circling the planet in silent waves?
Keys to epics, I hold these partisan details
that burn the writing hand
and pierce the eye's complacencies.

The Guide Recalls the Mountain

for Atul Dodiya

Every summer, they'd get off the train with their frayed knapsacks
and prop up their easels. They'd complain about the clouds
and dance on clear days when you could see right across
the bay, waves breaking on the silver sand like glass.
At the museum, you can see the mess they left behind:
the beach daubed in dots, the sky woven in stipples,
the sun blotted out by cloud-wool, and the mountain,
they painted this mountain so many times,
there's nothing left to see
except blotches of sienna and ochre.

You have to wait until the clouds wipe out the light
and the wind blows hard, impaling everything in its path.
Stand your ground: don't run halfway down the slope
to hide in the forester's hut.
Look, here's the ledge
where the painters always stood.
Lock your arms, stand up to the wind
and face north:
the peak stands cold and crystal-sharp.
It speaks to you when you squeeze your eyes shut.

Rehearsal for Departure

The quartermaster sits at his dusty table,
his singing breath anchored by ledgers.
He doles out the week's wages, fingers stained red.
It's ink, just ink, he reminds himself.

In his dreams, this outpost becomes a tropical island:
a tricolour sags at half-mast among the palms,
a nurse is sobbing, a surgeon has moulded
the death mask of a poisoned emperor.

A guard spits in the sand,
brushes a fleck of ash off the harbour cannon,
picks up his clove-scented eyeglass
to scan the sea for signs of invasion.

The quartermaster has the situation under control.
He has ordered the stagehands to lift
the catamaran from the sandbank
and float it on the agate water.

His porter has been waiting with a torn umbrella
that a lady bound for England dropped in haste
as she boarded the last ship out, when the Empire fell.
The quartermaster strides out on the deck

but keeps in the shadow of a tower crane
as he throws away the last of his ledgers,
feeds the gulls from a tray of crumbs
and clips on a pair of aviator glasses.

The docks go grey, the customs house goes black
but the ocean is a range of violets and greens.
He will adjust that as he goes, he tells himself,
flexing his fingers, still stiff from the desk.

A pilot is calling the time, the samurai wind
is shouting orders. The catamaran
has flung out wings. He salutes the flag
and switches on the ignition.

The joystick works like a song.
He hums as he takes off over the harbour,
leaving a thoughtful farewell wake
of bombs along the patchwork sea.

Enemy Action

The basin is a cool white oasis after nine hours on the trail.
A ghost is studying you from the mirror.
You rinse your hands, wait for his attention
to waver, then grab him.
He dissolves in a rain of scratches.
You stand there, holding a pair of black gloves:

an unshaved stranger in torn combat fatigues.

Night Runner

Divan-e Ghalib: Ghazal 191

The faster I run, the faster the oasis runs from me.
I'm fast, but the desert runs faster beneath my feet.

I'm running alone through the night, my heart on fire:
my shadow flies from me like a bird of smoke.

My feet grow blisters as I sprint through the desert of my
      madness:
I've left a trail of blood-pearls behind me.

Your face flashes from every facet of the cup of colours, a
      hundred faces:
they all become one again, in the prism of my eye.

Fire runs from that eye, that maddened eye:
it drips to the earth and sets the dried garden on fire.

Harbour Thoughts

Land is what you sight from a storm-broken ship,
the mirage they forgot to sink: you hold it
in your eyes, mouth clenched
around a flask
of brine.

Zameen
is where your ancestors
made landfall, measured off a site
between the mountains and the wash of the sea,
marked its boundaries with the king's horse-head seal.

Land is what you look for, all your life.
Zameen is what you hope to find.

The Afterlife of the Magi

The first is stunned by wind, lashed by breakers:
he covers a long distance in his mind,
leaves bloodprints on the shingled beach.

The second paces through a high-walled house of air:
its floor is desert, pricked with agaves
that root themselves in his heart, bleached milestones.

The third strides along a glistening coast, his cape a cloud
that hides him from the black boats knifing ashore.
The future fills his eyes, he cannot see

the bay's scimitar curve rising behind him.

The Empire of Lights

after Magritte

This house has not moved a brick since midnight.
Outside the front door, the streetlamp has brushed
the cobblestones with a moss of delay: the night
glows in a yawn between darkness and day.

The street flows on, soaking the canal
with brittle after-images of rain.
The bats that have chased butterflies of meaning
up the crescendos of trees all night

are drowsing in their green and icy silhouettes.
It is night here still, it will always be night:
this street is wound up tight to strike
at 3 a.m. and hiss a breath of doubt

into waxy clouds that are talking softly
about the ninja maestro who bled the clock dry.
They remember the day he parted the curtains
and broke the windows with his flame-coloured hands.

They are whispering about the jacarandas
that he drowned in the sky beneath the house
that has not moved a brick since midnight,
and how well cotton burns at noon.

Chimera

for Adil Jussawalla

Fear translation. The first verse grows
a red beak, a blade curved and fresh
as the mango it's about to bite.
The second whips open across the rustling page,
a pair of wings, all-weather kit, cased in steel
feathers, not wax. The third is a snaking tail, de rigueur
in futurist circles (this version isn't for now, you see,
but for after). So, mid-phrase, mid-sentence, a twitching sierra
on fire. Take a deep breath. Go to the fourth, which slices
what's left of the stalled air, a sleek black fin.
The eyes open last, and they will never look
at themselves in water. These amber-flecked lenses
are mine, on loan. They're strong enough to pierce
the walls and roofs of the floating mirage
we call world, and never turn to stone.

Fossil Curator

His fingers drum on mahogany, a beat coded in the bone.
Beneath glass, dawn birds come back to life from stone.

They raise their beaks to the mothball air, their wings
    creak and stretch.
Their eyes survey the parchment landscape in the blurred
    space of a breath.

The clock should have been ticking, but water's dripping
    instead.
These events are no less real for taking place inside a head.

His last hollow bone he leaves behind, the legacy of a flute:
among the mossy pebbles, a long and punctured fruit.

Lunch at Britannia

for Naresh Fernandes

I missed you by minutes at the restaurant:
it might have been your table, just vacated,
that the waiter gave me, with its plate
of berry pulao half-eaten, and bottle
of raspberry untouched, still sparkling.
A *nature morte*, titled 'Diner Called Away',
Chardin with a dash of Hopper, Morandi on the side:
a tableau painted by the crater of emergency
that makes a long-playing Pompeii of our works and days.
Is this a joke on me, the man who turned up late?
Or purest blasphemy, your immortal soul in peril,
accused by an empty chair?
You've defied

the supreme commandment
of Café Britannia, engraved on the menu in caps:
THERE IS NO LOVE GREATER THAN THE LOVE OF EATING.
That love, like its more elegant twin, the heart's appetite,
shall prevail. Hades' cup-bearers resolve themselves
into waiters with checked tablecloths, marching in legions
of order restored: they empty the remains
from ashtrays and volcanoes, clear away the relics
of bay leaf and fish bone. Stooped at his counter,
Mr Kohinoor smiles: At Britannia, there's life
after still life. The table is cleared and laid again.
With a fresh knife and fork, and a fresh order,
I complete your unfinished genre piece.

In the Margin of an Autumn Folio

for Nancy

Before the bell peals out and is heard in twenty-two languages,
before the shadows claim each pointed syllable for their own,
before the ocean explodes in every ripened shell in the world,
decipher this script, its tight-lipped serifs brushed with gold,
and pluck the one maroon flower, an amorist's clandestine trope
hidden among moulted leaves. Enclose me in your landscape.

Uses for an Executed Dissident

The skin is miles long when stretched out flat.
Flayed, you spread, your words invade
every peninsula gnawed from the borders
of the emperor's leached mind.
Dead, you talk to more people
than ever you did alive.

The imprimatur of summer rain
is stamped on this fertile skin that scrolls
in all directions like the untellable story,
slipping through checkpoints and barricades.
Just think, a clever doctor could turn you
into spiral-bound journals for children.

Or lampshades for people to wear as hats
on dark nights, going home from work.

The Soloist Performs with an Orchestra of Events

for Ranbir Kaleka

The greenest things happen when you're not looking:
creepers braid themselves around a bridge,
clouds surround a tower, nudge it towards a dead end
and neon measures the length of the cobbled street.
There's no one to hear you read, clearly it's time
to jump off the mind's cold waterfront

and follow the dolphins, whose dance lasts as long
as a notched breath, the naked spasm of a thought,
the yanking away of a hand. You could miss it
so easily and freeze. Is that you or a cut-out
parked in your chair? How wise to plant a proxy:
the greenest things happen when you're not there.

In the Garden of Departures

I spoke of beauty, she spoke of pain.
Around us, the cloud-lit monsoon sky
began to knife down in rain. A shifting wind
forced up a squall of birds and the garden gate
swung free of its hinges. She fought off my claim,
tearing at my sleeve, bright eyes strained.
At the broken bridge, when we stopped for breath,
the gate saw its moment, crossed its rusty arms
and signalled us to leave. The street had changed
into a swirling, eddying, impatient stream
calling for movement or a closing line.
You are not Kafka, it said, so get up and go.
We left the peacock's cry behind
like music lying unread on a score.

IV
The Existence Certificate

Checking the Toolkit

for Jürgen Brócan

You take things crafted by callused hands and name them
with words that bruise the tongue, graze the eyes,
that speak coarse fabric, grease, metal fatigue,
work's rough edge, sting of varnish,
knotted grain:

kerf, stroud, adze, spigot.

Spark these words
against other words, which damask
the whispering tongue, caress the grazed eyes,
naming beauty in syllables never moistened by sweat,
words that pluck and carve, bodied by loom, quill, brush:

brocade, palimpsest, persimmon, jade.

And repeat, as your words escape the prison of hands,
the reasoner's prayer: '*Brocade*: the eye following
a meander between banks of raised thread-of-gold.
Kerf: a cut made by a saw in a piece of wood.
A name for absence.'

Stroud, persimmon, spigot, jade.

Hunters tracking buried words, we ride
a stream of clouded light: its slowness rivals
the generations of cars that fly down the autobahn
hidden by plane trees, their sleepless tyres foaming
beneath our windows like an unseen ocean's tides.

Portrait of an Unknown Master

You've come to the coldest place:
rust peeling from tall trees
to settle in a fine powder on ice
that was river, bridge, mirrored cloud.

Stark paper, fine powder rubbed in its grain.
The face is red chalk dust
under the detective's fingernail.
Who were you?

The Strange Case of Mr Narrative's Reluctance

What shall I do with your silences,
master? Your grey eyes glowing
in a wall of sour cement,
the darkness in your blood,
your arsonist's handshake?

Shall I hold the girl running a hoop through the square,
grip the lighthouse looming at the end of the street?
Seize the shadow of the man puffing a pipe
as it lengthens on a hot brick wall?
Grasp the ivy that crusts on cool, high windows?

The water is crumpling in your hands.
Too much leaks into the world, you think,
too much. You are coming apart at the seams,
your buttons are going off like gunshots.
Let it spill, master, you cannot hold back

the goldfish exploding from your shirt-front.

First Lessons in Distance

for Annu

On the clearest January night one year in Fatorda,
my father taught me to thread the stars
with the needle of Greek legend.

Blackout paper still blocked the windows.
On the east coast, enemy soldiers were being marched
captive through mangrove swamps, under burning clouds.

But grenades and battle fatigues were alien
to my three-year-old eyes: unscarred by TV
and the reading lamp, they widened to hold

Rigel's blowtorch-blue edge and Aldebaran's red halo.
My father taught me to catch the fainter stars
by sleight of glance, from the corner of the eye.

Years later, standing beneath a Midwestern sky
(wide bowl, four jet trails blooming in it),
I remembered our needlework of pinpoint and name:

light-years away from earth, first lessons in distance.

The Hotel Receptionist's Confession

What could I do? I trusted them and they let me down.
They'd shamble in, flashing gawky legs, waving bony arms.
Or shuffle in crab-wise, bow-legged, too short
to sit at table. And there I was, thinking how poised
they'd be, how diagram-perfect, walking on air.

Believe me, it gave me no pleasure to tailor them to fit,
no pleasure at all. Imagine the horror of breaking ankles,
chopping hands at the wrist, stretching ligaments
until they snapped, or trepanning a slice of skull.
I had to do it all. But it was worth every minute, it was.

You have no idea how beautiful and transparent
a little blood makes the world, how perfect.
And how else could I have got them
to lie in comfort on my flawless bed?

Base Camp of the Lost Expedition

Beware the pent-up heaviness of traces.
The tent has vanished, thread by thread,
leaving only a flap to flutter
between two loud oceans of air.

Behind it, in the space
that was once behind it,
the needlepoint wind
has filigreed a still life

with scattered melons, rusted knives
and, stunned by an anglepoise lamp,
a coffee mug standing on the coaster
of its own shadow.

Call the event into question,
summon each version
to the witness stand.
This dryness belongs

to a strip of skin
torn from the desert's thigh.
The rain trembles
in the airspace on the other side

of a sealed border.

The Memoirs of Don Quixote

for Dilip Ranade

Portrait of a Stranger

I heard a stranger in a black cloak
aim a spell at the windmills:
the clouds reeled over the horizon
in wounded squadrons.

The dervish was dancing on the wind,
his stick grown into a leafy sword.
His head was flying by itself
among the bloodied clouds.

How soon will it melt, this burnished sky,
the stranger thought as he paid his tab.
His belt uncoiled on the innkeeper's table,
a snake ready to explode.

When he trotted out of the courtyard,
his horse neighed as if to shirk off
its weight of rusting armour,
as if it dared disturb

the peace between a sleeping lance
and a saddle buckled to carry
the nomad's lonely whistling.

Bull

A bull thinks about the silver towers of a chemical plant.
A philosopher among bulls reflects on a fortress of capital.

Beyond the binary of plant and animal, a third:
in the distance, out of reach
of the animal's horns and the plant's surveillance cameras,
a snatch of landscape.

A place of low hills with a single star
suspended in the sky,
the horizon receding in veils of purple and viridian:
a setting for the birth of the Promised One.

The bull is versed in scripture.
He will know the magi when they come.

The Green Shirt

Write to me tonight. What must a man do
when delusion prompts him
to go in search of himself?

Look, he's just a green shirt
ripping itself open
in the shape of a clown.

'I am no more than the sound
of a man going to pieces,'
Ghalib wrote from his sickbed.

Look, look at his reluctant feet:
the quicksand has
claimed them.

Hand

That hand. Surely, sir, you saw it move?
Surely you saw it clench

like a hairclip clutching at vanished hair,
like a velvet crab scuttling out of water

on the way to its next victim.

Dog

What is that dog doing under the no-moon sky?
Here, the wingless fly and the winged ones
fall to earth.

The man with the halo
is nursing a headache
and missing his wings.
He stands alone in a field
of blood, waiting for rain.
A shrill crow perches
on his halo.

But the dog, as I was saying: the dog
has put his muzzle into a man's mouth
and is probing it.
Dr Dog, I presume?
Well, don't. Not yet. It's possible
that the man is trying to bite the dog
with his toothless mouth.

Stranger things have happened.
Those entrails draped on an armchair, for instance,
are what a man is when you strip him down to essentials.

Frog

Take a radioactive frog.

What happens when you split him wide open?
A flapping accordion to demonstrate
bifid symmetry (such perfection!)
for the taxidermist's pleasure?

He turns out to be a frog with impeccably Modernist,
not to say Theosophist, tastes.
His insides: red, white, a quadrilateral or two,
blue, black bar, yellow, black double bars.

The croaking of a crumpled Mondrian.

Birdsword

A rain of sabres is falling gently
on a parliament of geese
and on a man standing among them.

The man rips his chest open in slow motion:
rib by rib, each rib a sword.

The field in which he stands
assaults him with a tide of mud.
His stripped body meets the field

with a burst of song,
blood's only resistance.

The rib-swords are growing feathers.
The geese are flapping
and a rain of sabres is falling gently.

Man Weighed Down by Halo

Dogs, more dogs: augurs of war to Caesar's ghost,
their muzzles pointed at the sky,
their howls piercing the stars' ears.

And the man weighed down by his halo, the saint man, he also
looks up with them, awaiting a sign.

Is he in exile from that glimpse of a landscape
with its single star? That serai we passed when we passed
the silver towers with a thousand eyes?

The Curator in His Labyrinth

The curator finds his footprints in every corridor and annexe,
every cupola, rotunda, pergola and gallery he finds.
He knows this is not the orderly museum
that glows at night in catalogues.

This labyrinth grows with every thought he thinks,
every word he mouths and every breath he takes
as he circles through it.

He will not abandon his labyrinth.
He is its curator.
Etymology commits him to duty's nuances.
He must take care, he must care for, he must be careful,
    he must care.

Cave Canem, Caveat Curator

Beware of dog, curator beware.
The halo and the rib-sword are everywhere.
Open your mouth and let them burn your speech,
let the dervish welcome the magi, the frog share its grief
with the hand grasping at the green shirt's collar
and yourself, healed by jagged fragments, slip out

through History: the broken gate, the now and forever
breach.

Late Lunch in a Besieged City

The cashier's in shock. He'd dragged out
the striped awning, expecting rain:
a metal peacock's fan. Now it's lying
twisted on the ground, the windows
are shattered, the tables shrouded

in sheets of the finest broken crystal.
Beheaded men are walking through the smoke
towards us, and ambulances are wailing like voices
hunting for the throats that have abandoned them.

But nothing can derange the ephemeral moment,
which will die only by its own hand
at a time of its own choosing:
an army of firemen could not clear up
the drop trembling on the chilled lip
of the beaker, the crumbs resting on the plate,
the fish bones heaped neatly to one side,
the shiny orange left for a later
that's just been postponed indefinitely.

Hymn to the Stranger

You are invisible. No cloak, no halo, no staff
to single you out among the crowds
that surge at daybreak as you slash a path
through their murmured prayers, trailing a wake
of puzzled pilgrims who felt a brief shock pass,
touching their caps or sleeves, leaving in the air
a whiff of sulphur, a hint of camphor, the lightest
tremor of clove. And where the hand can bear
the pressure of your gauntlet, you press hard,
leaving the man to cry out, marked by his friends
as mad, an ecstatic dowser of unseen springs,
a lute for unvoiced harmonies. You do not wait
to see what use they make of your gifts, the people
you touch. Some, wide awake, fan the day with torches,
others fall asleep on their feet, every corner they turn
a blind corner in a labyrinth echoing with buskers.
You're a step ahead of the fastest, a shade behind the slowest,
grenade in one hand, cyanide vial in the other,
you are destroyer, you are redeemer,
now shrewd, now negligent, one eye on the score,
one eye on the moving finger that keeps the score.
Hour without name, you swim beneath the days of others:

when you surface and your hand comes out of the duffel bag,
some get paper roses, some serrated throats, others hear no more
than the inconsolable cry of an extinct seabird.
You hack through the streaming-plankton crowds
as they pray for your advent: never looking back,
a torpedo, invisible.

The Secret Agent

Joseph Beuys (1921–1986)

A thought that has died inside him leaks out
as a stag streaking across a page, its horns
skewed by the grain, and the nymph
he cannot catch by sight alone is dressed
in night's sparkling haze and he must lunge
at her hair, her breasts, her thighs with graphite
stabs, his hands breaking into antlers,
his mouth a snout rooting in the black earth
for scents his mind has lost on the trek
to the scribe's carrel, and now the margin of thought
is red again with the ribs of the roasted stag and washed
with the mixed gold and blood in which he's drawn
the nymph on a chair, who watches him twist and fall,
shake himself free from his tangled, muddy pelt:
comet-maned, meteor-eyed, throat belling with wolf-howl.

The Navigator's Last Entry

Paradise is a narrow waterway
and the clocks on board are dripping wax
on maps mottled with new islands.

Grow fins. You have a week to spare
before climbing the reef.

Revised Passenger List

The ship is filling up very nicely
with those who were never counted:
the artist-philosopher makes place at his desk
for the plantation slave and the hawk-eyed Sultan,
the explorer gathers up his satin cloak
so the bird-crowned Emperor of the Spice Islands can sit,
and the Duke of Whatnotburg has to squeeze in a bit
for the pepper trader whose sweat has dried
to fine salt on his ebony skin,
tidal Malabar exchanged
for canalled Venice.

This ark is seriously overloaded,
the captain tells the first mate.
You can bet your last dinar
it's going to be tough
to get the *Renaissance* to sail
on this particular voyage.
New rules in the book, but will the vessel haul?
It's funny, but they took up no space at all
in the hold of the *Memory*. No one told me,
not even the lost novelist we saved from the wreck,
that ghosts weigh so much when you pump them with colour.

Documentary

Light boxed in a square, the dark tidal against us.
Word-wings whip at our faces in a wind of no story.
I tax your loyalty to a rudderless friend.
This isn't film, I stage-whisper, it's footage.

The Enemy's Country

From end to end the tide rips the crescent beach,
tears up barbed-wire fencing, splits brickwork shells.

The painter on the watchtower has felt the sun's injustice.
His back on fire, he paints the high wall a defiant red

as though to welcome an invasion. It comes
riding a broken line of waves, drumming the rocks.

From all points of the notched compass
the atolls growl landward.

Fern

This feathered leaf must have fallen from the hand
of the woman who turned around to see
if her child had strayed too close to the slope
of the fuming mountain or the hunting birds,
and left her footprint in ash that hardened
to rock. A spray of seeds released that noon
remains in the thick air, and this gift:

a leaf trapped between layers of mud
that volcanic fire baked into stone.
Drained of light and green, long spasm,
breath dusted with pollen:
a net of veins splayed on an altar
where the river turns in its sleep
and an old woman lights a lamp.

Reading a Script at Ziarat Dastgir Sahibun

Srinagar, 2005

Proverbs fall from the saint's upturned bowl.
Beneath the cypress, work is a steel-grey word,
thought is plum and prayer a mournful green.
A cube with three lacquered walls and a broken face
holds them together.

The almond merchant shuffles past the lake
without humming. The singer hides his voice
under a scarf. The guide won't admit to his compass.
They're actors in a long-running movie about comets,
in which a pair of hands wash themselves at a fountain

over and over, the soundtrack worn out, silence dripping
from the stripped chinar and the charred roof
to the headstones buried in snow.

The Myth of Eternal Return

Fatorda, Goa

You leave the megaphone on the beach
and nature to its own devices,
tread sand, paddle across clumped seaweed
and speak to the road, watched by latticed eyes.
Palm green is the colour of asylum here, and sleep
comes quickly in its shade. Here's where you rest
from the water that burned your hands at noon.
But rest is hard work, every turn seems wrong
and where the chapel stood, a rusting sentry points
to a lane that climbs among houses, and no hill.

Your words grow lean and spare when breath
is crafting ways to temper a slope.

The croton leaves that speckled the wall
are ash, but the east windows still give
on the bamboo grove. Trying the gate,
you look along the leaf-swept drive.
The woman bending over Caesar's grave
is the girl who raced you up the hill
(she won, you fell and have a scar
on the forehead to prove it).
You wait for her to turn.
It's me, you say, after all these years.

Botany

Prickly garden where voices flower and run to seed:
this conversation could go up in a sheet of flame
any time, any leaf could be a bait, any tendril
a booby trap. Watch your words, and hers, theirs,
and all your stranded thoughts. Clove and mandrake
open the mouths of your mind, all dialogue here
is rolling transcript for a police state:
check the names for shadows, the verbs for stains,
turn connoisseur of signs, yogi, give nothing away
except your deep-shelved archive of silences.

Interior, South Avenue

There's never enough light
by which to say: Write.
The word's brevity does not strike
this trembling hand with the deadly poise
of a commandment.
I sketch in silence, helot of an eclipse

that lifts when my fingers find
a starfish of candle-wax on the table
and your maroon hairband on the pillow,
a flower in the warm pit that remains
after you've woken up and left.
Sleep's drifting edge, and just enough light
by which to say: Write.

The Magician's Field Notes

This apple has goodbye written all over it.
The north tower is yesterday, that green lamp post is now.
My bowler hat? Sure. At your own risk.
And about my lion, you can whistle till the clouds come home
but he's just lurched off a stone ship
and won't be standing up when the door yawns.
Speaking of which, our beach is a harvest of anchors,
the tide a staircase that's lost its way.
My umbrella's so wet, it's fireproof by day
but what do I call the shoe that fizzes
in my heart all night?

Try asking the angel rooted to the bridge,
shoulders hunched in thought,
watching the months glide past on salmon wings.
Out-of-work acrobat, he's thinking on his feet
in the homeland of reversible errors
where this bridge is a fatal exception:
it won't take him home again.
That leaves the river.
God, yes, this papyrus barge could float
but someone must push it out before it sails
and no one knows where the wind-tuner's got to.

V

The Institute of Silence

Fulcrum

Camille Claudel (1864–1943)

The old man has gnarled, enormous hands that drip wax.
He can break you down to muscle and set free
the naiad hiding behind your mask.

He can trap you in a tree that's barely broken
the rippling surface of marble
or melt you down to a river of bronze.

His kneading, curious fingers have found
the greatness that crouches inside you.
His hands mould it in a tight grip.

He lets go only years after he's pulled you apart,
wounded you where it glories the most.
Your last studio: the rolled foetal drawings

fall open. Your body still hinges
on where he is, leaps out
in five directions at his touch.

Spoor

How to move in the other's skull follow the spoor the
other has tracked over days of grass acorn freshet mud
how to smell the roast ox warm crust the other has
smelled how to mull on the river the other has swilled to
sink from hills to parched watercourse to flow into the
lake he saw to growl in the other's belly roar through his
mouth find the trace this pugmark this scratched deodar
yourself you leave behind and running you turn and hear
from the hills your own last howl

The Calligrapher's Bequest

All green has gone from the broad chestnut leaf
pinned behind glass: a fan of dried veins
with the name of God brushed across it
in swirling currents of gold.
One of a thousand hopes, all thousand mixed in each.
My shadow falls across these dancing strokes
and evaporates. The slant afternoon light is raining
through the barred panes, through the eclipse of my body,
on this dead leaf that carries the most beautiful word.

Countdown

Dortmund

I've painted a door on the wall
for the wind to gallop through.

A ginger tomcat sits on the stoop,
waiting for the parked lorry to drive away.

The last of the moths are clinging
to the blackened roof, which shrugs them off.

I'm painting the numbers back on the clock.
My origami swan is ready to fly.

Bihzad Closes His Eyes

for Peter Weibel

He sits in the centre of the carpet of silence, the last of all the carpets he will sit on, and calls out to the trees by their special names.

Cedar was always good to him, wrapping its fragrance around his books. Cypress offered him the shelter of love. Pine shielded him from angry princes and jealous slaves. Poplar kisses his windows. Willow sweeps his river clean. Every autumn, *chenar* has covered his garden with leaves like hands of flame. These he has trusted. But today they are quiet, respectful, distant.

And his colours? He has fought them through the long dream of his life, powdered them in the mortar of his heart, glued them with anger. They have stung his sleeves and bitten his gold-leaf borders. He has dragged them across marbled pages with his brush, forcing them into images.

God made man from clots of blood. A painter makes saints from broken coral, grinds emperors from lapis. While other men sleep, he barters queens for turquoise. Spies bring him crushed cinnabar to finish his tented cities. Traders find him leopards and peacocks to draw. No cabinet is safe from his fingers: he will claw through the flasks and retorts of friends, looking for the lost elixir.

Who called him an idle collector of travellers' tales? He listens. He knows every shade will open in its own time, tell its story in the fall of stained syllables.

But Bihzad has not listened to his colours for many years. He has forgotten the boy who beat off the swans and read the deepest pages of water. He has forgotten the young man who slashed through afternoon's sawdust shrubs and the green silk pavilions of evening, the wolves howling in his blood. Too soon, he came down from the mountains and chained himself to the forced march: an album for the king's uncle, a portrait for a merchant, love spells for a princess, the chamberlain's prayer book. To the beat of the sun's hooves, he herded his colours through the gates of floating palaces and honeycombed bazaars. Splashed them on stairways left unfinished when the barbarians attacked, steps locked between earth and heaven. Hurrying north after the retreat, he dripped his colours on sketches that soldiers threw into winter fires, watching them shrivel into veils of ash.

On this last carpet, he does not whip them with strokes of ink or trap them in porcelain cages. He knows the black angel is coming for him in a rain of sand, gardens and houses crumbling in its eyes. Nothing stands between Bihzad and the angel except his colours. He draws his shawl around his shoulders. Once again the song of an open wound, he chants their names: *laleh, kermes, sikarlat, khun-e siyavush.*

Dragon's blood blesses his page.

For Example

The saint maintains his piety through the graphic imagination of other people's vices. We thank him for it.

The saint's impossible perfection allows us to go on being gargoyles while keeping our faith alive. We admire him for it.

The saint's silence covers far more than our interpretations of it.

The saint has stood in the cave of light. He has spoken to the spirits of trees. His poetry is the fan of the white peacock opening against the rough shrubbery of our speech.

Authorized Version

The true believer has lost his touch.
His world is an album with its pages torn out.
His past is a field of marble testaments.

There is ash at the roots of his stormy hair
and salt in his blood.
Who taught him

to hide in crowds,
to plant steel pomegranates
in children's eyes

and drip poison
on the beehive of words?

The Poet in Exile

Paper that's a decade old tears easily.
Recall: it used to be the skin of a tree.
It shreds along folds, frays around words
from which the surging breath's been bleached.

Reason and beauty should have no enemies,
I used to say: they go everywhere, their time
is an effect of love. But I've seen them end
in bonfires, warmed my bloodless hands

and watched as universal ideas crackled,
sparks glinting off crumpling bevel and spine.
I've outrun the charred patience of saints,
the torched wit of sophistry.

The rivers are shallow here, but who says I'll swim?
I'll count the fish and stop complaining
about the narrow bed, the sputtering lamp
and your profile in ink, instead of you.

I've got used to the screeching parakeets
that southern traders prize, the fleas of sweaty horsemen
and their rough-haired dogs, the stench of chained bears.
At night I dream I'm tearing up my letters.

Forests die quietly as the pages catch fire.
The flames play across my chalky walls
and river mist kills my windows.
I wake up wearing a halo of leaves:

my own laureate, my own hangman.

The Nomad's Song

Don't judge me by this keel-hung boat
on which the river has printed its sleep.

Judge me by the thin red line that glows
where my finger ends and the sky begins.

Pilgrim from before the harsh logic of the plough,
I cultivate my mirages.

The horizons trail in my mind
like watered silk.

Brancusi in Indore

You've been here before. You've walked to the edge of my memory.

Brancusi comes to Indore, dreaming of a shrine. His patron is always escaping his plans.

He crafts a walled pool to mirror the sky's eye. The pool ripples out on paper. He smells frangipani. The landscape settles in his camphor cabinet.

He crafts a flock of birds for the shrine. They test the sky, shoot through the clouds, balance the monsoon on their feathers, and return to his rough-gloved hand.

Under the sculptor's roof, it is always summer. White as sand in a cold eye, the birds never migrate, not even when the snow begins to drift through his sleep.

Native Informant

We've caught a trace of the moment's passage: the stain spreading on this page, a twist of ink, machine oil or deer's blood. You say you can record it?

Are you good at describing your own people and customs, dragoman? Or do images drive you mad? Do you press cloves of fantasy between the pages of science? Will you recite parables when we ask you for geography? What's accuracy to you?

You speak two tongues but work at the Institute of Silence. Do you know the lanes that connect the scriptorium to the marketplace? Can we trust you to attend to voices outside your head?

We'll be watching you closely. You're writing the future's memory.

Insomnia Station

I'm waiting for the parrot to close his red eyes so I can close mine.
My current project is sleep.
I'm wrestling with the formal problem of sleep.
I'm teasing out the nuances of sleep.

I'm in a permanent condition of attempted recovery:
always at number four in the holding pattern,
circling above your city,
unable to land.

Zwartewater

Utrecht

The true wheel fights the mill-race:
without curb or brake, it fires up and turns
not with but against the crested, foaming rush.
I part the tangled curtaining creepers, half afraid
to meet the roar, take the spray in my face
and clutching at the blistered rail, look, really look
deep into the fray, where a ladder, seamed and scored,
singes the swirling green with its daubed blue.
Which I grip, giddy with glory's call or ruin's final spin:
mad as a hermit handed a lost bible of prickling skin,
I wade out to the wheel, in the milk-wash to my knees,
my thighs. Lion-roar fills my ears and I
burst from myself in the sluicing, leaping rush.

Revolution

As the soldier's sister, who saddled shadows,
she rode through the dark, grey dappled on grey,
ringing her bell.

As the farmer's wife, who chopped garlic and diced carrots
against the clock, she had the best practice of all,
watching the guillotine fall.

As the priest's mother, she hung up her laundry
on a line sagging between sand-pitted columns,
picking head after head from her basket.

As the swan girl, she polished the bronze horses
every summer till they sweated against the colonnade,
printing their heat on her baby's cradle.

And her hand, this hand that is writing:
you can slip it off any time you like
and try on another silk glove.

Immersion Technique

It's nearly noon and you're still balancing on the diving board, wondering how and when to break the mirror. The blue's on fire. Ripples circle out from a ring someone's thrown in. Don't count on them to ease your plunge.

The pool is as deep as you can go.

Tidemark

Bombay, July 2005

Water draws a line around the things we loved.
I pluck dead birds from the wash and burn their feathers.

This is where I belong, in tidal water
drawn up over my feet like a shell blanket.

I hate this city on the sea, but I will die here.

Plumb Line

The voice doesn't always empty itself in words.
Where the pen settles and sinks its blue squirt
a trace is sent down miles, through deep latitudes

to the glowing other shore of the plumb-pierced earth.
There, the lilt of a song you heard hummed as a child
still bells out of a throat, and a clay-mottled hand

pulls at a blue-veined porcelain knob to shine
light on an echoing fall of steps, down which
you wade, palms feeling for walls, and hear again

the words that breath made the first time you sank
in the warm bay, feet scrunching sand that slipped away
from beneath them, called back by the running tide:

the sky filled your eyes, your hands grabbed at starfish
stuck in slime, your hair sparked on the trawling wave
and the sun's wings brushed your lips.

Incision

Lucio Fontana (1899–1968)

Cut quickly. There's sky behind the flesh.
Prise up the fold. The atlas of the body is never complete.

Crossing the Heart of a Continent

for Axel Fussi

Your hand scuttles across the page, the landscape cruises past.
Something beautiful is waiting to break
in hard weather. Somewhere, yellow pods are bursting.
Somewhere, the glissade of eighteen musicians.

Steeples queue up to question the afternoon's testimony.
We pass the thicket where you buried your shadow.
Now scatter these pomegranate seeds
that I've traded with you for a skull.

Cross this plain before the blackbirds wake up and cry.
The train skirts a barricade of hills
and glides through the gauze of evening light.
Fingers scrabble at ivory knobs, old voices screech.

Who's speaking? You're travelling in a trap.
The stands of fir are priests frozen at mass,
the road signs flag the tombs of autobahns.
In this museum, the war has never ended.

Your hand grows crabbed in the cold
but you cannot stop the train in the middle of a poem.
Let the lines run on, past the bay horse in the field,
the lightning-hit steeple, the white gate.

The open book of the sky burns very slowly.

The First and Last Portrait

Put on these wings. You never knew where to stop
and lapsed into lucid self-awareness only rarely.
This is the last rendering, the closing of accounts.
The charcoal stops here, after this nothing will matter:
your betrayals will be proof of love, your rages
omens of a sublime intensity.

This is the first and last portrait. After this
no questions, after this you can shed
the mantle of affection, the scarf of duty.
You can be all madness and insomnia,
you can hover above this town of barking dogs
like an eclipse. You can become a god.

Acknowledgements

I would like to thank the editors of the following journals, in which a number of the poems included in this volume first appeared, sometimes in earlier versions:

Bengal Lights (Dhaka); *Boulevard Magenta* (Dublin); *The Caravan* (New Delhi); *Coldnoon: Travel Poetics* (New Delhi); *Fulcrum* (Cambridge, Massachusetts); www.fieralingue.it (Bolzano); *The Green Integer Review* (Los Angeles); *The Indian Quarterly* (Bombay); *Nether* (Bombay); poetry.sangamhouse.org (Bangalore); *Prairie Schooner* (Lincoln, Nebraska); and *Westerly* (Crawley, Western Australia).

I wish to thank, also, the editors of the following journals and periodicals, where some of these poems have been published in German translation:

Akzente (Munich); *Neue Zürcher Zeitung* (Zurich); and *Die Zeit* (Hamburg).

Acknowledgements are due, as well, to the editors of the following anthologies, in which a number of these poems have appeared:

Both Sides of the Sky: Post-Independence Indian Poetry in English (ed. Eunice de Souza; New Delhi: National Book Trust, 2008); *The Harper Collins Book of English Poetry* (ed. Sudeep Sen; New Delhi: HarperCollins, 2012); *These My Words:*

The Penguin Book of Indian Poetry (eds Eunice de Souza and Melanie Silgardo; New Delhi: Penguin, 2012); and *Another Country: An Anthology of Post-Independence Indian Poetry in English* (ed. Arundhathi Subramaniam; New Delhi: Sahitya Akademi, 2013).

A number of the poems included in the present collection have appeared in German translation in Ranjit Hoskote, *Die Ankunft der Vögel* (translated by Jürgen Brôcan; Munich: Carl Hanser Verlag / Edition Lyrik Kabinett, 2006).

A few of the poems in the fifth section of *Central Time* have appeared, in earlier versions, in *Pale Ancestors* (Bombay: Bodhi Art, 2008), an artist book on which I collaborated with Atul Dodiya, and which collated forty-eight watercolours by Dodiya and forty-eight of my poems.

I would like to thank the organizers at the many venues where I have read from these poems:

The Frankfurt Book Fair (2006); Literarische Gesellschaft/ Café Vetter, Marburg (2006); Lyrik Kabinett, Munich (2006); Marmorsaal, Nürnberg (2006); Deutsch Amerikanisches Institut, Heidelberg (2006); Prithvi Theatre, Bombay (2007); Literati Bookshop, Calangute, Goa (2007); Hausacher LeseLenz, Hausach (2007 and 2012); Goethe-Zentrum, Hyderabad (2008); Chemould Prescott Road, Bombay (2008); the First Dubai International Poetry Festival (March 2009); the First Munich Literature Festival (November 2010); Poetry with Prakriti, Chennai (December 2011); the Goa Arts and Literary Festival (December 2011); the Galle Literature Festival (January 2012); the Jaipur Literature Festival (January 2012); the Emirates Airline Festival of Literature, Dubai (March 2012); the Hyderabad Literary Festival (January 2013); and the Kala Ghoda Arts Festival, Bombay (February 2013).

I wish to record my special thanks to my editor at Penguin, R. Sivapriya, for her sage counsel, warm support and unflagging patience; and to Richa Burman for the collegial sensitivity and attentiveness with which she has copy-edited the text. My grateful thanks are due, also, to Maria Hlavajova and Arjan van Meeuwen, as well as Dorine Sneep, Marieke Kuik and my other friends and colleagues at BAK/basis voor actuele kunst, Utrecht, for a period of residency during Spring 2013, which gave me the repose to complete work on this book.

The quotation that acts as epigraph to this book is taken from Richard Sennett, *Together: The Rituals, Pleasures and Politics of Cooperation* (London: Penguin Books, 2013), p. 213.

As always, I wish to thank my parents, Chandra and Raghuvir Hoskote, for their love and for their gift of an abiding sense of belonging, which sustains me at home and away, translates continental distances into neighbourhood walks.

This book is dedicated to its first reader, without whose love, constant support and critical responses it would not have begun its journey into the world: my wife, Nancy Adajania.